17 party pieces for cello and piano

Alan Bullard

CONTENTS

The Associated Board of the Royal Schools of Music

2·95

21·98

2

Clog Dance

ALAN BULLARD

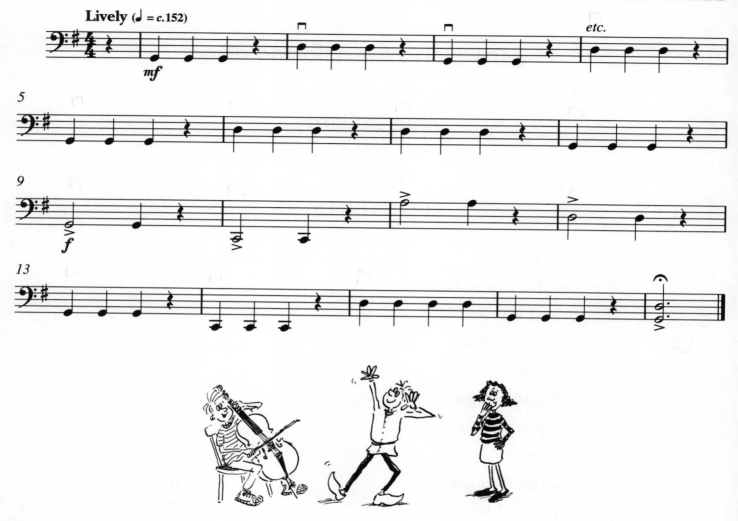

At the Castle Gates

AB 2576

Cool Blues

Medium blues tempo (♩ = *c.*100)

* The piano part is notated in 12/8

Rock the Boat

Country Walk

Bluesy-boogie

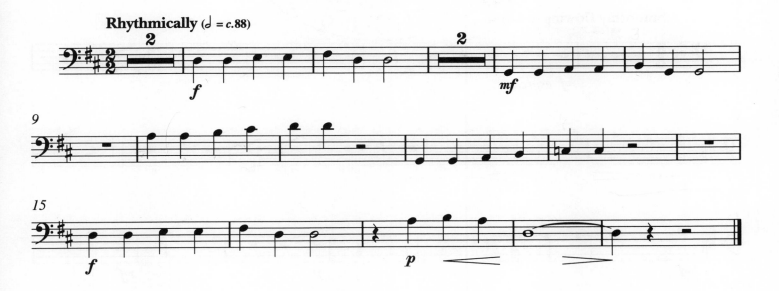

Top-string Latin

Lullaby

In the Groove

Graceful Waltz

Far Away

Square Dance

Rhythmic Rumba

See-saw

Day-dreaming

Hungarian Dance

Jazz Waltz

Printed and bound in Great Britain by
Caligraving Limited Thetford Norfolk

PARTY TIME!

17 party pieces for cello and piano

Alan Bullard

CONTENTS

The Associated Board of the Royal Schools of Music

Clog Dance

ALAN BULLARD

AB 2576

At the Castle Gates

Cool Blues

Medium blues tempo (♩. = c.100)

* pizz.

mf

* The cello part is notated in 4/4

Rock the Boat

Country Walk

Bluesy-boogie

Top-string Latin

Lullaby

In the Groove

Graceful Waltz

Far Away

Square Dance

Rhythmic Rumba

See-saw

Day-dreaming

Hungarian Dance

Jazz Waltz

Printed and bound in Great Britain by
Caligraving Limited Thetford Norfolk

AB 2576